DATE DUE

Simple Machines

What Is a Pulley?

By Lloyd G. Douglas

Children's Press®
A Division of Scholastic Inc.
New York / Toronto / London / Auckland / Sydney
Mexico City / New Delhi / Hong Kong
Danbury, Connecticut

Photo Credits: Cover and pp. 5, 7, 13, 15, 21 (upper left), 21 (lower right) by Cindy Reiman; pp. 9, 21 (upper right) © Kevin Fleming/Corbis; pp. 11, 21 (lower left) © Michael S. Yamashita/Corbis; p. 17 by Maura B. McConnell; p. 19 © Annie Griffiths Belt/Corbis
Contributing Editor: Jennifer Silate
Book Design: Mindy Liu

Library of Congress Cataloging-in-Publication Data

Douglas, Lloyd G.
What is a pulley? / by Lloyd G. Douglas.
    p. cm. -- (Simple machines)
  Summary: Introduces pulleys and how they work to raise flags, as well as heavy objects.
  ISBN 0-516-23961-9 (lib. bdg.) -- ISBN 0-516-24024-2 (pbk.)
  1. Pulleys--Juvenile literature. [1. Pulleys.] I. Title.

TJ1103 .D68 2002
621.8'11--dc21

2001047539

Contents

This is a **pulley.**

A pulley is a rope wrapped around a wheel.

5

When the rope is pulled, the wheel moves.

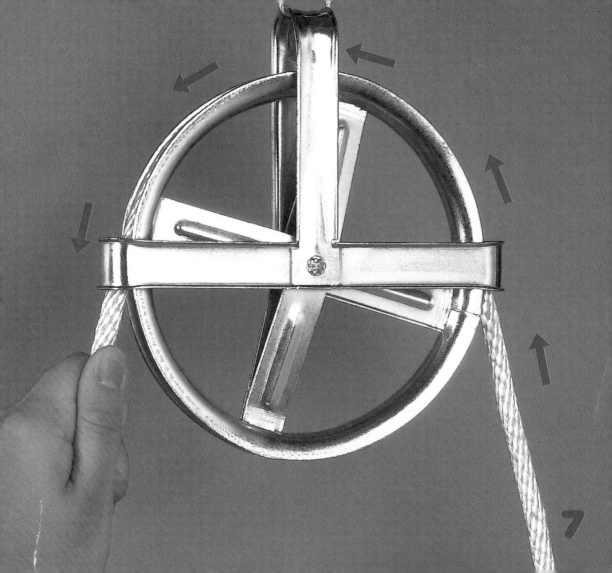

People use pulleys to make work easier.

Pulleys can help move things that are hard for people to move.

Pulleys are used in many ways.

These people use pulleys to help them cross a river.

A **crane** uses pulleys.

Can you find a pulley on this crane?

There are pulleys at the top of the crane.

They help people lift heavy things.

4500LBS

1000/6=DM

15

A **flagpole** also uses a pulley.

17

The flag is put on the rope.

People pull the rope to raise the flag high.

Pulleys are very important **simple machines.**

20

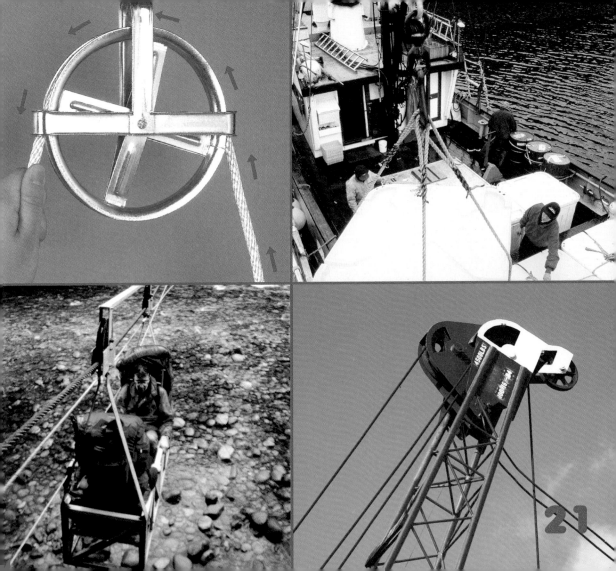

New Words

crane (**krane**) a machine with a long arm, used to lift and move heavy objects

flagpole (**flag**-pohl) a tall pole made of wood or metal for raising and flying a flag

pulley (**pul**-ee) a wheel with a grooved rim in which a rope or chain can run

simple machines (**sim**-puhl muh-**sheenz**) basic mechanical devices that make work easier

To Find Out More

Books
Pulleys and Gears
by David Glover
Heinemann Library

What Are Pulleys?
by Helen Frost
Capstone Press

Web Site
Spotlight on Simple Machines
http://sln.fi.edu/qa97/spotlight3/spotlight3.html
This Web site has lots of information about pulleys and other simple machines.

Index

About the Author
Lloyd G. Douglas is an editor and writer of children's books.

Reading Consultants
Kris Flynn, Coordinator, Small School District Literacy, The San Diego County Office of Education

Shelly Forys, Certified Reading Recovery Specialist, W.J. Zahnow Elementary School, Waterloo, IL

Sue McAdams, Former President of the North Texas Reading Council of the IRA, and Early Literacy Consultant, Dallas, TX